stay up to
speed

performance management
for decision makers

GW01388411

FORMAT
PUBLISHING

Published by
Format Publishing Limited
9-10 Redwell Street
Norwich
Norfolk NR2 4SN
United Kingdom

www.formatpublishing.co.uk

First published 2003
ISBN 1903091357

British Library Cataloguing in Publication data
A CIP record for this book is available from the
British Library

This publication *Stay up to speed: performance
management for decision makers* is based upon source
material which is either Crown copyright and/or Crown
copyright with value added product status. Such
material has been reused and refocused under licence
from and with the kind permission of the Controller of
HMSO and the Office of Government Commerce.

Cover illustration: *Men jumping hurdles* by SIS
Ltd/Bruno Budrovic
Other illustrations by Digital Vision

Printed in the UK by Norwich Colour Print on paper
derived from replenishable forests maintained with
'two-for-one' planting

contents

1

introduction

- What is performance management?
- Why manage performance?

there is pressure to perform everywhere. Individuals, teams, departments and entire businesses are all expected not only to perform at a certain level, but to raise that level over time. But how do we know when we are performing well?

What is performance management?

Performance management is the activity of tracking performance against targets and identifying opportunities for improvement. With it, you can move beyond an intuitive sense of 'how you are doing' to a more objective, analytical approach.

Performance management is about gauging success: whether targets have been met, goals achieved, and changes made smoothly. Unless you look at performance, your knowledge of what has been achieved is incomplete, and therefore your understanding of what has to change is inadequate. So performance management focuses on what has happened in the past, but it is also about the future – how can you do things better, what targets should be set, what needs to change?

Performance management can be a vital tool for informing management decisions and is a key to organisational learning. At a basic level, performance management is a driver for efficiency: 'what gets measured gets done'. Good performance management promotes efficiency and good business practice, hopefully without imposing inappropriate targets that distract from key objectives. However, performance management also encompasses more strategic concerns: the performance of teams, departments or an entire business. At these higher levels the focus shifts from measurements of volume or profit towards gaining a sense of how much progress has been made towards long-term goals.

This guide presents the basic concepts of performance management, from building a performance framework to choosing performance measures that work, setting realistic targets and putting the framework into operation.

managing performance is about managing for results

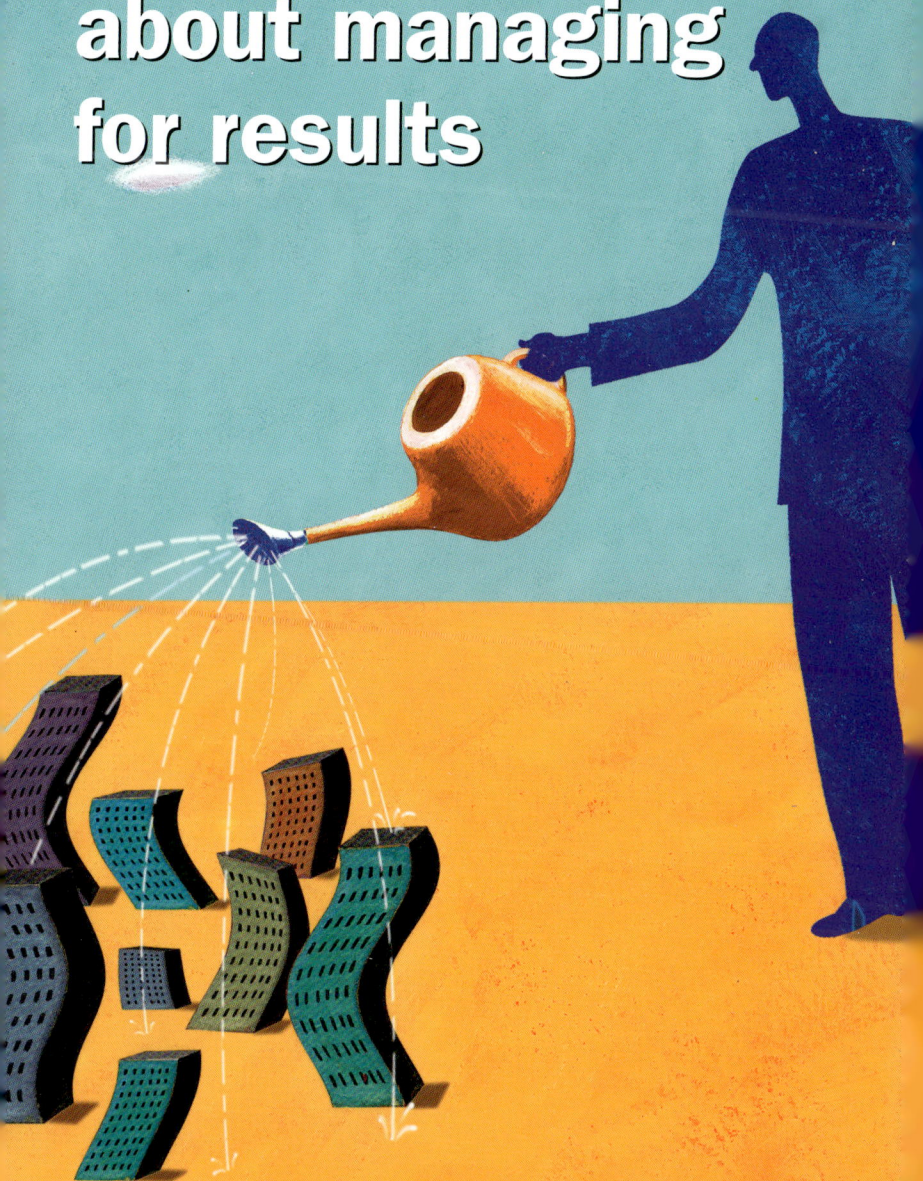

Why manage performance?

Managing performance is about managing for results. It is not an academic or theoretical exercise. It means defining what constitutes success, finding out whether it has been achieved, and taking action to remedy problems.

Performance management can:

- tell you whether you are meeting objectives
- reveal problems that bias, emotion and time can cover up
- through performance measures and targets, provide a common language for planning and reporting throughout the business, and on the benefits realised through change
- provide an early warning of problems, and an indication of how effective the responses to them have been
- give you more time to prepare for fluctuations in demand or workflow, personnel changes and other resource issues
- inform management decisions
- give vital feedback to staff, customers and stakeholders on the quality of products and services
- by making achievements (and failures) visible, make effective accountability possible.

There is a great deal of truth in the maxim 'if you can't measure something, you can't manage it'. Basing management decisions on performance information implies that:

- you know what you are aiming for
- you know what you have to do to meet your objectives
- you know how to measure progress towards your objectives
- you can detect performance problems and remedy them
- you can determine whether you have the right objectives and when to change them.

2

overview

- Levels of performance management
- The cycle of performance management
- Inputs, outputs and outcomes

Whatever the area of focus, the elements of performance management are broadly similar. The stages, and the questions that each one involves, are shown on the diagram, which represents performance management as a cycle of activities. The questions to be answered at each stage are covered in more detail in the following chapters.

Levels of performance management

Performance management operates at three levels: strategic, business and operational. The highest level is the assessment of your success in achieving strategic goals – asking questions such as:

- are we moving towards our high-level objectives?
- are we moving towards them quickly enough?
- are we delivering the outcomes that we should?

Answering these questions will require supporting information from the lower levels of performance management.

The questions that performance management at the business level seeks to answer are:

- what should we be measuring, and how?
- how can we set targets and provide incentives that will improve quality and not distract from key objectives?
- how can we do better?
- are we getting value for money?
- what is an acceptable level of quality for the services we provide?
- how can we ensure that we meet our business objectives?
- should we be aiming for continuous improvement?

Performance management at the operational level often involves statistical or mathematical analysis: the precise weighing of costs against outputs and the quality of those outputs. This is the simplest level of performance management, but also a vital one. It deals with questions such as:

- are we meeting our targets?
- are we attaining the desired level of quality?

Origins

What are we trying to achieve?
What constitutes success?

Building a performance framework

What processes and outputs do we need to know about?

Review

Did we find out what we needed to know?
Should we redefine success?
What can we learn from this?
Did we realise the benefits we wanted?

Choosing a performance measures

What will be measured?

Using performance information

Have we met our targets?
How can we improve?

Setting targets

What levels of performance are acceptable?
Should performance improve over time?

Performance monitoring and measurement activity

What's happening now?

Defining processes

Who will collect the data, and how?
What will that cost?

- could we do more work in the same time (improving efficiency)?
- could we do our work better (improving effectiveness)?
- could we save money (improving economy)?
- how are individual staff performing?

Inputs, outputs and outcomes

Performance management is not always an exact science, but it should still aim to be as objective as possible. One way of doing this is by thinking in terms of inputs, outputs and outcomes. These terms are often used in performance management.

Inputs are the resources that contribute to the production and delivery of an output. Many inputs can be expressed in, or reduced to, financial terms. Some examples of such material inputs would be:

- raw materials, consumables, overheads and running costs
- expertise – technical, managerial, procedural or legal
- staff – newly recruited or redeployed from elsewhere
- staff training
- financial investment
- policies, procedures and standards
- infrastructure, equipment and premises.

Examples of less tangible inputs, or those that are harder to express or quantify financially, include:

- management time or commitment
- motivation and enthusiasm
- positive, proactive or sympathetic management attitudes
- positive business culture.

Outputs are the products, services or conditions produced by the business. Outputs can normally be measured numerically or as proportions. An output can also be a state to be maintained: availability of a service, for example.

Examples of outputs include:

- products made
- projects completed

what outcomes do you want?

- enquiries dealt with
- proportion of time a service is available
- turnover and profit.

Outcomes are the highest level of output: the strategic aims of the business. They are the real-world results of the business's outputs combined. Desired outcomes express the aims of business activity at the highest level. Creating the desired outcomes is the final test of success or failure, and success at this level usually implies success at other levels: if all the desired outputs are produced, then high-level outcomes should be realised.

Realising outcomes normally depends on achieving a number of outputs, and is also affected by the business context. So it is not always possible to make a link and prove conclusively that an outcome has actually been realised as a result of achieving outputs. That is because measuring success at this level is often subjective: outcomes cannot normally be expressed as numbers.

Examples of outcomes include:

- restructuring or transforming the business
- moving into new areas; opening new market sectors
- improving quality of service to customers
- providing services to customers in radically new ways
- redefining the culture of the business
- enhancing the business's reputation or public image.

Inputs, outputs and outcomes can interact in many ways. There may be outputs that are dependent on other outputs for their production, or that form the input for another process. For example, if everyday business operations are made more efficient, time is freed up to work on innovative new projects and change the business for the better; achieving a tangible output results in a positive input to the business, which in turn produces a desirable outcome.

3

building a performance framework

building a performance framework means deciding which processes, activities and outputs in your business need to be examined and then selecting a range of performance measures, perhaps of several different kinds, that combine to give an accurate, balanced picture of them.

Building a framework is necessary no matter what your focus. You may be seeking to assess the performance of the whole business, a small department, a team, a contract or an individual – the attributes of a good performance framework are the same regardless of scale or scope.

Setting up a performance framework is as much an art as a science. It may prove difficult without prior knowledge of how the framework will work in practice, or how useful the information it produces will turn out to be. To some extent, what you find out later can shape the evolution of the framework: while constant changes to it will be counterproductive, nothing needs to be set in stone. To help at the outset, learn from the experience of others wherever you can.

The choice of performance measures to fill out your framework is absolutely crucial. The measures you choose will govern what you can and cannot know about the business, and the range of measures you select will affect the balance of your perspective. Measures that are relevant at the outset may become less so as the business evolves, and will need to be revisited. It also important to set baselines (see chapter 4), from which to assess improvement.

Understanding business processes

This is the first and perhaps the most important step in building a performance framework. Some processes and activities within the business are more important than others. You will need to identify those that are critical and those that are less so. This will help you decide what needs to be measured.

The questions you need to ask here are:

- what goals are we trying to achieve?
- what are the core products or services that are helping us (or could help us) achieve those goals?

which business processes are critical?

- who are our customers? Do we want more, or different customers?

- what are our main business processes, and what supports them in their operation?

- what flows of materials and information are involved in those processes?

Note that 'customers' could include other departments or teams within the business.

To fully understand a business process, it is worth analysing it in terms of its inputs and outputs, and the relationships between them; it may be helpful to create flow diagrams and flowcharts. Remember that the output of one process may form the input for another, or two business processes (perhaps in different locations) may work together to produce an output.

Try to analyse the intangibles too. Does a department depend on the enthusiasm, knowledge or drive of a particular individual (intangible input)? Is the success of a particular team generating a positive feeling of achievement (intangible output)? Don't make the mistake of regarding these 'soft' factors as irrelevant to rigorous business analysis. A framework that neglects the human side of performance cannot hope to make all-round improvements or involve people in the process.

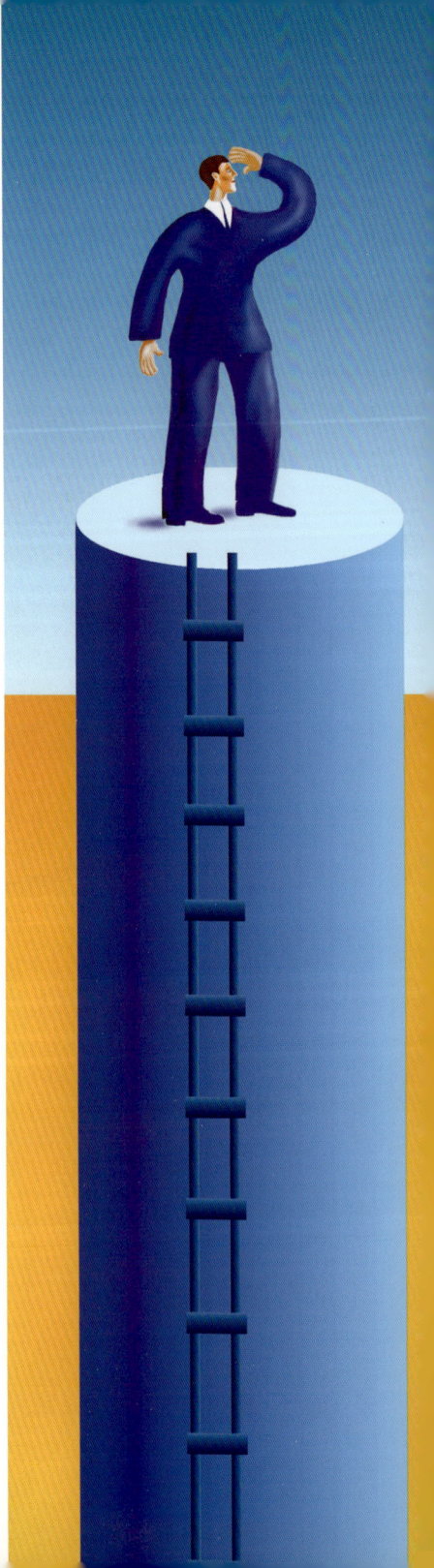

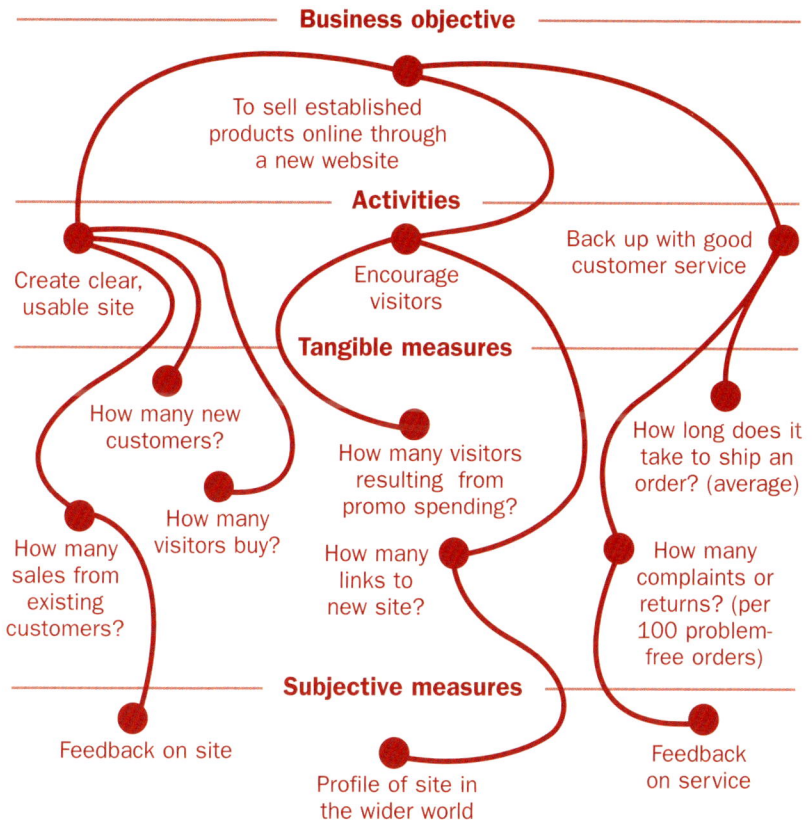

Business objective

To sell established products online through a new website

Activities

Create clear, usable site

Encourage visitors

Back up with good customer service

Tangible measures

How many new customers?

How many visitors buy?

How many sales from existing customers?

How many visitors resulting from promo spending?

How many links to new site?

How long does it take to ship an order? (average)

How many complaints or returns? (per 100 problem-free orders)

Subjective measures

Feedback on site

Profile of site in the wider world

Feedback on service

Cascade of strategic objectives

Although many performance measures, by their nature, often reflect events 'at the coal face' of the business, it is important that they are all linked to strategic objectives or outcomes. Applying this principle to the selection of measures should ensure that they reflect those activities that are important to the business as a whole. It can also help to focus actual business effort on things that really do move the business forward, rather than offering incidental or opportunistic benefits that do not truly contribute to the 'big picture'.

The diagram gives an example, based on the provision of an e-commerce service by an established business, of how high-level objectives can be cascaded to performance measures for which business units, teams or individuals can take responsibility.

building a performance framework

Measures can be defined by working down the cascade from objectives to measures. A starting point is to ask 'why are we doing this activity?' The answer will depend on the level in the business at which the question is asked. At the highest level, objectives and the reasons for them will generally be defined in terms of strategic business aims ('sell products online'); at the lower levels they will be expressed more in terms of outputs ('increase number of customers by 10%').

The next questions to ask are 'how can we tell if we are meeting this objective?' and 'what information is needed to enable us to make informed judgements about the success of the activities involved?' The information may be easily quantifiable or it may be harder to pin down (for example if the aim were 'to raise the profile of the business'). Whatever the nature of the information, it will start to suggest ways in which you can quantify success through performance measures.

The value chain

One way to express the relationship between inputs, outputs and outcomes is in terms of economy, efficiency and effectiveness: three distinct areas in which performance can be measured, linked together through the value chain (shown in the diagram). Each link in the chain has a direct influence on the next, and measures of economy, efficiency and effectiveness focus on how these influences operate. A balanced performance framework, particularly one with a focus on a department or an entire business, will need measures of all three kinds. Carefully choosing measures allows you to trace how the building blocks of financial savings and efficiency gains enable benefits at higher levels in terms of achieving the aims of the business.

- **economy** measures express the relationship between resources and inputs (the cost of inputs)
- **efficiency** measures express the relationship between inputs and outputs (how good performance is with the given inputs)
- **effectiveness** measures express the relationship between outputs and outcomes (outputs' contribution to high-level strategic business aims).

Improving economy and efficiency means analysing the relationship between resources, inputs and outcomes. This will help to determine how inputs can be changed to improve outputs: more staff, better equipment, better management, or other changes. If nothing can be

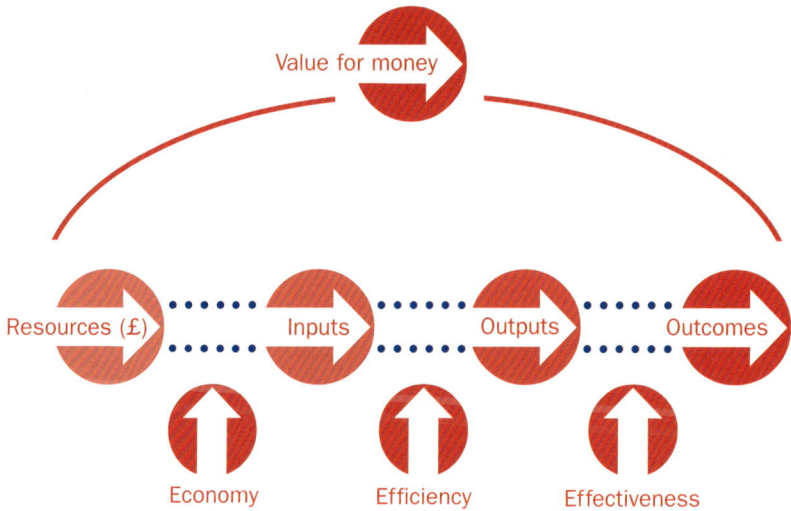

Value for money

Resources (£) → Inputs → Outputs → Outcomes

Economy   Efficiency   Effectiveness

done to improve outputs by changing the inputs, the process itself may have to change: new business models, different suppliers, new directions.

An analogy here is the sausage machine: if the outputs of the machine (the sausages) are unsatisfactory, you have the option of changing the inputs (varying the ingredients), altering the process (tweaking the machine's settings) or transforming the process (buying a new machine of a different kind). A good performance framework can survive transformation, providing a continuous 'before and after' picture of performance in times of radical change. In other words, it uses measures that are applicable and comparable both before and after the change.

Outputs combine together to create outcomes. If outputs are as good as possible, but outcomes are not being achieved, it is time to ask not whether the business is doing well enough, but whether it is doing the right things.

An overarching concern at all value levels is value for money, which links the highest levels with the lowest. Achieving value for money does not necessarily mean making cost savings. In fact, it could mean making significant investment. Essentially, it is about realising outcomes through the best use of resources. Achieving value for money means moving beyond simple questions of 'what does it cost?'

or 'how much profit does it make?' to a more sophisticated analysis of exactly what contribution to the business ia made by resources and investments of all kinds, at all levels.

A balanced performance framework will include measures of quality as well as quantity. The relative importance of the three areas depends on your area of focus, but no area should be neglected completely. To put this another way, even the most basic measure of what something costs should be linked somehow to the aims of the business.

As well as outputs or outcomes in business terms, the quality of management processes should also be measured. This might involve assessing the way you do things with established models of best practice.

Finally, it is important to remember that outcomes do not happen in a vacuum. There will be contextual influences, and these will have to be taken into account when analysing performance information (see chapter 5).

Economy measures

Economy measures aim to answer the question 'what does it cost to carry out this process, or manufacture this product?' They focus on the cost of acquiring inputs; the emphasis is on achieving value for money at the most basic level. Optimising economy means minimising the cost of an activity while maintaining quality.

Some examples of costs are:

- **one-time costs:** the costs of setting up a process, including IT investment, the purchase of premises, consultancy fees, and so on

- **unit costs:** costs incurred on a per-transaction basis, for example a fee charged every time a particular service is used, or the cost to produce and sell a single manufactured unit

- **recurring costs:** costs incurred on a regular basis, for example a flat fee charged every month for rent, or a particular service used by the business

- **internal costs:** staff time cost, accommodation, facilities required, and so on.

Economy measures are likely to take the form of a financial ratio, such as a 'cost-per-transaction' or 'cost-per-time-period' figure, rather than a simple measure of absolute cost.

stay up to speed

Efficiency measures

Efficiency is the relationship between outputs – goods, services or other results – and the inputs used to produce them. Measures of efficiency look at whether a process maximises output for a given input, or minimises input to a given output. Measures in this area concentrate on how many times a critical activity has been carried out, or how many critical products have been produced, for a given level of input. They are the most concrete and easily quantifiable performance measures. Some examples of efficiency measures are:

- number of units manufactured in a year
- number of sales completed in a month
- number of customer enquiries, as a proportion of the total, that led to new business
- increase in productivity resulting from (say) investment in IT.

are you moving towards your goals?

Effectiveness measures

Measuring effectiveness is about determining whether all critical business processes are working together to achieve what you set out to do. Effectiveness measures focus on the relationship between outputs and outcomes: how well the outputs of processes or activities within the business are contributing to its overall success.

Examples of outcomes include:

- increasing market share; moving into new market areas
- acquiring another business, or disposing of part of the business
- providing services or marketing products in new ways (online, for example)
- radical restructuring, expansion or contraction of the business
- far-reaching business change; fundamental reappraisal of where the business is going.

Effectiveness measures aim to assess how well you are doing such things, or to what extent you have achieved them.

As well as high-level outcomes, you may want to look at intermediate outcomes. These are significant achievements that do move the business forward, but still represent a step along the road to greater things. For example, if moving into a new area of the market means you need to recruit a new team, the successful completion of their recruitment might be seen as an intermediate outcome, while successfully expanding your market focus is a key business outcome.

Another perspective on this, therefore, is that intermediate outcomes often relate to the business itself and its internal workings, while high-level outcomes have the wider scope of the business's interaction with its environment. This means that measures of effectiveness are, by their nature, complex, and also the most subject to contextual influences. They are also the most subjective of measures, since success at the highest level can be difficult to express through statistics or ratios.

At higher levels of performance measurement and management, businesses often define key performance indicators (KPIs). As the name suggests, these are indicators (often not precise enough to be described as measures) of success in key areas. Achieving them will constitute partial or full realisation of strategic aims.

The emphasis at this level of performance management is likely to be as much on learning lessons as on finding areas for immediate improvement. The time that elapses between gathering the information and using it for improvement is likely to be much longer than with economy or effectiveness measures.

Quality measures

As well as 'how much' or 'how many', you will also need to measure 'how good' – the quality of the outputs or processes. Attributes that could be measured to assess quality include:

- usability or usefulness
- attractiveness
- accessibility
- flexibility
- accuracy
- availability
- turnaround time, or processing time
- error rates or defect levels
- cost of repair work done under warranty
- conformance with standards.

Some of these measures (such as accuracy) relate to the quality of outputs from a process, and others (such as conformance with standards) to the quality of the process itself. This distinction may equate to a difference of focus between 'good' performance as your customers understand it, and 'good' performance as other stakeholders (auditors, shareholders, etc) understand it.

Hard, numeric measures are always the ideal, but some quality aspects can be very difficult to quantify and their measurement has to be subjective. Usability and flexibility are good examples; by definition, an assessment of these attributes is going to be partly or completely subjective. Time also lends perspective. As data accumulates, subjective questions can become more objective simply because of the weight of evidence.

Subjective aspects should not be neglected simply because mathematical techniques cannot be applied to them. Other techniques, such as surveys, may provide data that can be analysed. It is a question

stay up to speed

of gathering information and analysing it with as much objectivity as possible. For the framework to be balanced, some imprecision or even uncertainty in the framework may be inevitable. This does not mean it gives an unreliable or misleading picture; quite the opposite. It would be wrong to imply that all aspects of performance are empirically and immediately 'knowable'.

A balanced performance framework should include all relevant quality measures; what 'relevant' means will have to be agreed between everyone involved. Ideally, this definition would not be affected by the problem of subjective measures, but in the real world you have to balance the need to assess all aspects of quality with the pragmatic issue of what is actually measurable.

What is worth measuring?

The resource put into collecting performance information should be proportionate to the benefit the information brings. Resources include the cost of taking measurements, but the time burden imposed by requests for information is also a factor, as well as the time taken by managers to review performance information. Unless you have staff dedicated to managing performance, time spent on it will be time not spent on business activities. This does not mean that performance measurement is irrelevant, indulgent or an optional extra, just that a balance has to be struck.

Allocating resources to performance measurement may have implications beyond the business as well; for example, if you expand your focus to include the performance of your suppliers. You do not want requests for performance information to affect the services you receive, or sour the relationship with your suppliers, but it may be essential to look at the kind of value you are getting from suppliers, for example by benchmarking prices.

The possibility of using existing data sources should always be considered. There may be information already available that could fit the purpose. You may need to consider how (or whether) your existing information management systems support performance management, and how they contribute to management decision-making in a wider sense. Benchmarking (see chapter 6) could be a way to use other businesses' data sources for improvement.

Proxy measures

To quote Einstein, 'not everything that counts can be counted; and not everything that can be counted counts'. Often the most important performance factors are the hardest to quantify. For example, it may be difficult or impossible to express feedback from customers numerically, but their views on quality will probably be a vital part of assessing performance.

It may be that measuring something that is quantifiable can give you a 'handle' on a much less tangible aspect. Such a measure is known as a proxy measure, since it acts as a substitute for a measure that cannot easily be created. For example, an indication of 'staff morale' may be provided by a measure of staff turnover rate. The assumption is that there is a correlation between the measure and the less measurable phenomenon that lies 'behind' it.

When analysing and presenting the results of proxy measures, remember (and remind others) that they are built on assumed relations between different aspects of the business. Take care when using proxy measures in drawing conclusions, making strategic decisions, or linking them to incentives. Retain a focus on what is 'behind' the proxy measure, or you may find you are focusing efforts on changing the proxy rather than the reality.

How many measures?

A few basic, well-aligned measures taken seriously are better than a large number of complex measures that fail to clarify anything or inspire anyone to improve. There should be no more performance measures than are necessary; don't waste time and resources gathering information that is interesting but not directly relevant. Questions to consider include:

- is it generally agreed that this activity or process needs to be watched closely, and action for improvement taken if necessary?

don't use too many measures

- should it be continuously monitored for improvement?
- does the activity relate to customer satisfaction and the quality of our service, or is it purely an internal one?
- is the benefit of measuring performance in this area worth the cost of taking the measurement?
- can the impact of the activity be determined or directly attributed?

One way to look at this is to ask what action could be prompted by the performance information. There is little point collecting disappointing performance measures only to find that nothing can be done to improve them in any case; the cost of taking the measurements could probably be better spent elsewhere.

the performance framework must be balanced

A balanced framework

Performance measures should give a balanced overall picture.
Frameworks that focus on one area are likely to lead to unmeasured
activities being neglected. This can happen when measurements
focus on what is easily quantifiable; quantity rather than quality,
for example.

An unbalanced performance framework, with gaps or biases in its
coverage, may result in perverse incentives or promote the wrong kind
of behaviours or attitudes. For example, measuring the quantity of
query letters answered but not the usefulness of the responses may
clear a backlog but at the expense of a quality service.

Working with key stakeholders – those involved in the activities being
measured, those doing the measuring, and those who will use the data
– can help to ensure balance.

Ready for change?

The performance framework
should be able to withstand
change. It should be able to show
you the benefits of changes you
make within the business. It
should also endure through
changes in personnel and not be
dependent on the knowledge,
skills or influence of a single
individual or particular group.

Ideally, it should also not depend
on a particular business process,
so that if you do the same
activities in a different way, comparable performance data can still be
collected. This may be very important if it is necessary to measure
performance before and after a programme of radical change, and to
make 'before and after' comparisons that are like-for-like and
therefore meaningful in judging success. Changes in the definitions of
measures should be avoided where possible, to maintain comparability
across the change. Using standard definitions, where they exist, may
help in this. Standard definitions also provide a useful common
language within the business.

Avoiding perverse incentives

The act of measuring something often changes the behaviour of those affected by the measure. Measures must not create perverse incentives – that is, encourage behaviour that exists to meet a target rather than to improve. Well-chosen measures will reinforce the right behaviours, improvements and changes, rather than working against them.

An example of a measure with a perverse incentive is a measure of the speed in answering letters that is not balanced by a measure of the quality of the responses. The way information is used may cause perverse incentives too; for example, if performance-related pay is linked to performance measures that do not give enough weight to the quality of the work done, or its benefits to the business as a whole.

Focusing measures directly on objectives, rather than intermediate processes, can help to avoid perverse incentives. Measuring outputs instead of outcomes, for example, can discourage a positive attitude to change, or encourage people to cling to old ways when new ones could lead to better outcomes.

What makes a good performance measure?

The right performance measures will vary depending on the business and the focus of performance management. In general, performance measures should be:

- well defined
  - clear and unambiguous to avoid misinterpretation and ensure consistency
  - easy to understand by everyone who uses them
  - credible enough to be communicated to others, within and beyond the business
- focused
  - linked to business strategy, or to results higher up the value chain
  - linked to the needs of customers
  - appropriate and useful for the people who will use them, and developed with their involvement
  - able to suggest actions for improvement

stay up to speed

measures must reflect the business accurately

- accurate, reliable and verifiable
- open to comparisons and analysis
- timely: producing data regularly enough to make it possible to track progress and take action.

Roles and responsibilities

If the performance framework is to operate effectively, and not be left by the wayside, you must be clear about who will do what. The key responsibilities are:

- collecting performance data
- comparing measurements against targets and reporting problems
- setting or approving targets, and making changes to them
- deciding what action to take to improve or restore performance.

In practice, two or more of these tasks might be carried out by a single person. For example, a simple performance management process might be implemented by two members of staff: one to collect data, compare against targets and report to a manager, who sets targets, allocates resources and manages the process.

Communication

Communication is a key factor in gathering information. Once responsibilities are defined, it is important that all involved feel confident in the information flows involved; that their information is being used constructively, that problems can be raised if required, and that they are fulfilling a useful role.

Communication will help to co-ordinate the various tasks involved in performance management, speeding up the flow of information and helping to iron out any glitches in the performance framework and the task of putting it into practice. Informal means of communication, such as group meetings, seminars and 'brainstorming' sessions can all help people to feel more able to raise concerns and communicate openly with others who are involved.

stay up to speed

4

setting targets

- Types of target
- What makes a good target?
- Specific
- Measurable
- Achievable
- Relevant
- Timed
- The baseline
- Continuous improvement
- Key questions for setting targets

targets are quantified objectives. They express the goals of the business and provide the basis for identifying problems and moving towards solutions. Defining a target answers the question 'what are we aiming for?'

Types of target

Targets take different forms, depending on the context. They can focus on any stage in the value chain, from inputs to outcomes. To assess the performance of the business as whole, you will need several targets, at different stages in the chain. Often, meeting targets at lower levels is a vital, enabling step towards meeting higher-level targets. Generally, targets are more precise and mathematical at lower levels of the value chain (economy, efficiency) and become more subjective – but no less real – at the higher levels (effectiveness).

Some kinds of targets, with examples of each, are:

- fulfilling a binary (yes/no) measure, often within a set timescale:
  - service available
  - product introduced
  - changes to the business carried out
  - standards complied with
- achieving a set level of input:
  - costs reduced to a certain level, or by a percentage year on year
  - staff turnover kept below a specific level
- achieving a set level of output:
  - specified number of queries answered
  - specified number of sales made
  - service available for a specified proportion of the time
- achieving a set level of quality:
  - queries answered within a specified time
  - number of complaints below a specific level

- realising intermediate outcomes:
  - new systems improve efficiency of internal processes
  - internal business processes transformed
  - culture of the business transformed or improved in specific areas
- realising strategic outcomes:
  - moving into new market areas
  - significant growth in business volume, turnover or profit
  - business transformed through acquisitions or mergers
  - public image of the business radically improved.

Outcomes such as increased turnover are relatively easy to define targets for; setting targets for outcomes such as changing business culture and improving public profile may be more difficult.

Intermediate outcomes are high-level results that represent a 'stepping stone' to strategic outcomes; for example, moving into a new market area might depend on first transforming internal business processes.

targets should be both realistic and challenging

Successfully achieving the first target is a vital step towards achieving the second. The intermediate outcome in its turn will depend on the achievement of many other output and input targets further down the value chain.

Performance targets may be defined locally, to suit the situation of particular departments or teams, or they may be defined at the business level. Targets that are generally understood can provide a useful common language within (and even beyond) the business, but on the other hand, individuals and teams must be able to relate to their targets and feel that they have control over achieving them.

As with measures, it is important to choose the right number of targets. Too many can be counterproductive, and increase the risk of conflicting targets.

What makes a good target?

Targets express the desired or necessary level for performance measures to reach, surpass or maintain. The way they are expressed reflects the measure (or measures) to which they relate. At the simplest input/output level, setting targets is about specifying a minimum numerical value for a measure, or the value that it should attain after a certain period. For quality measures, or those that relate to outcomes, the target may not be so easily quantifiable.

Setting the right targets is just as important as selecting the right measure. It is crucial that targets are realistic (not a management 'wish list') but at the same time challenging for those involved.

Good performance targets will be SMART: Specific, Measurable, Achievable, Relevant and Timed.

Specific

Targets should be clear, unambiguous and easy to understand by those who are required to work towards them. Clear and specific targets promote common understanding of aims as well as consistent data collection.

Subjective assessment may play some part in performance measurement, but targets should be as specific as possible. If targets are hard to quantify, the definitions of the terms used to describe them are crucial and should be agreed between all stakeholders. For example, terms such as 'satisfaction' and 'milestones' are open to different interpretations and may have to be precisely defined for the specific context.

Measurable

It must be possible, or become possible in the future, to demonstrate that targets have been met. This means they must be specified in a form that is directly related to the relevant measures, and compatible with the way in which measurements will be made. Gauging whether targets have been met should involve a minimum of 'translation', evaluation or consideration of performance data. To establish that improvements have truly been made, you will need to show objective, impartial evidence.

There is no point setting a target for which success cannot be gauged by direct reference to a specific measure or combination of measures. This is particularly important for targets at the higher levels of the value chain: effectiveness targets, or those relating to outcomes. Showing that strategic targets have been met should not be about assertion, assumption or opinion. It should be a process of building up a pyramid of targets that have been met, with each level demonstrably enabling achievement at the next. Consider the effect on stakeholders of a perceived division between the levels. It could create a rift between those accountable for targets that are a concrete, quantifiable everyday reality, and those further up the hierarchy whose targets come to be regarded as far more slippery and subjective.

Also avoid the trap of setting targets for which you will not have adequate information, or you will be unable to prove whether or not they have been achieved. In time, they will come to undermine the perceived value of performance management in your business.

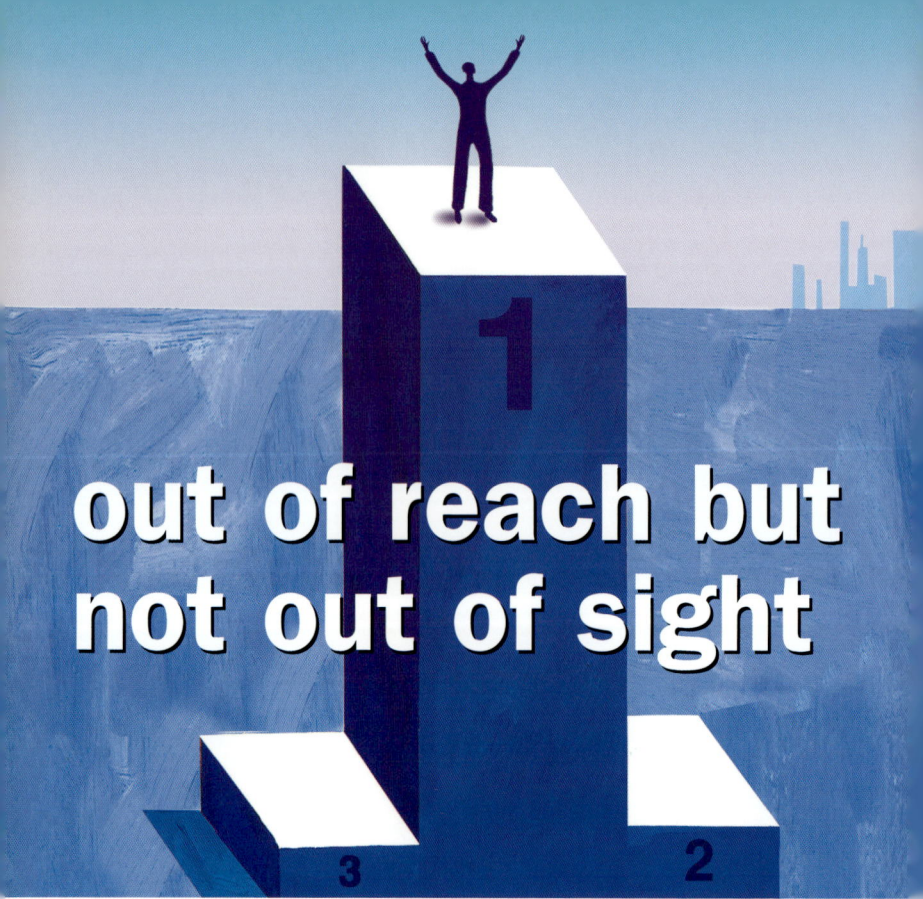

out of reach but not out of sight

Achievable

Targets, whatever their scope or level of focus, should express specific aims that people feel can realistically be achieved with reasonable effort. They should be 'out of reach, but not out of sight'.

Achieving a target must sit comfortably with existing business processes and the way people work now, to avoid perverse incentives. Targets that overemphasise certain areas while neglecting others may put such pressure on staff that their normal activities become distorted – possibly to the overall detriment of the business. People should feel that targets relate to their responsibilities and priorities, and that they are not pushing them in the wrong direction or distracting them from 'real work'.

Targets relating to inputs and outputs carry some danger of imposing pointless obligations on capable staff. Such targets need to be chosen carefully so that they do not constrain people's ability to find solutions and make decisions on what constitutes value for money, quality of service or immediate priority. If you oblige them to spend time meeting a low-level target, they could neglect the more important ones higher up. Setting a target that leads to sub-optimisation may worsen rather than improve overall business performance – as the adage suggests, 'people do what you inspect, not what you expect'.

Relevant

Targets must be relevant and appropriate to those who will be required to meet them, at whatever level in the business. People must have control over the factors that influence meeting their targets, or their motivation will suffer.

It is important that targets are more than rigid requirements handed down without explanation. People at all levels are more likely to feel motivated by the performance framework if they are able to identify the impact of their efforts.

People should ideally 'own' the measures and targets they will be working with, and should be able to understand and accept the validity of measures and targets at higher levels of the value chain. There should be clear links between overall measures of the success of the business and individual measures of success. If people are fully involved, they can bring their detailed knowledge to bear on the definition of measures and data collection processes.

The way in which information is presented can also have a significant impact on the way in which managers – and senior managers particularly – understand performance information, and 'buy in' to the findings.

Timed

There should be a set timescale or period for achieving a target. Open-ended targets may not encourage focused effort on improving performance. It should be made clear that performance will be assessed when the set period has elapsed, and that targets and measures will be open to review at that time.

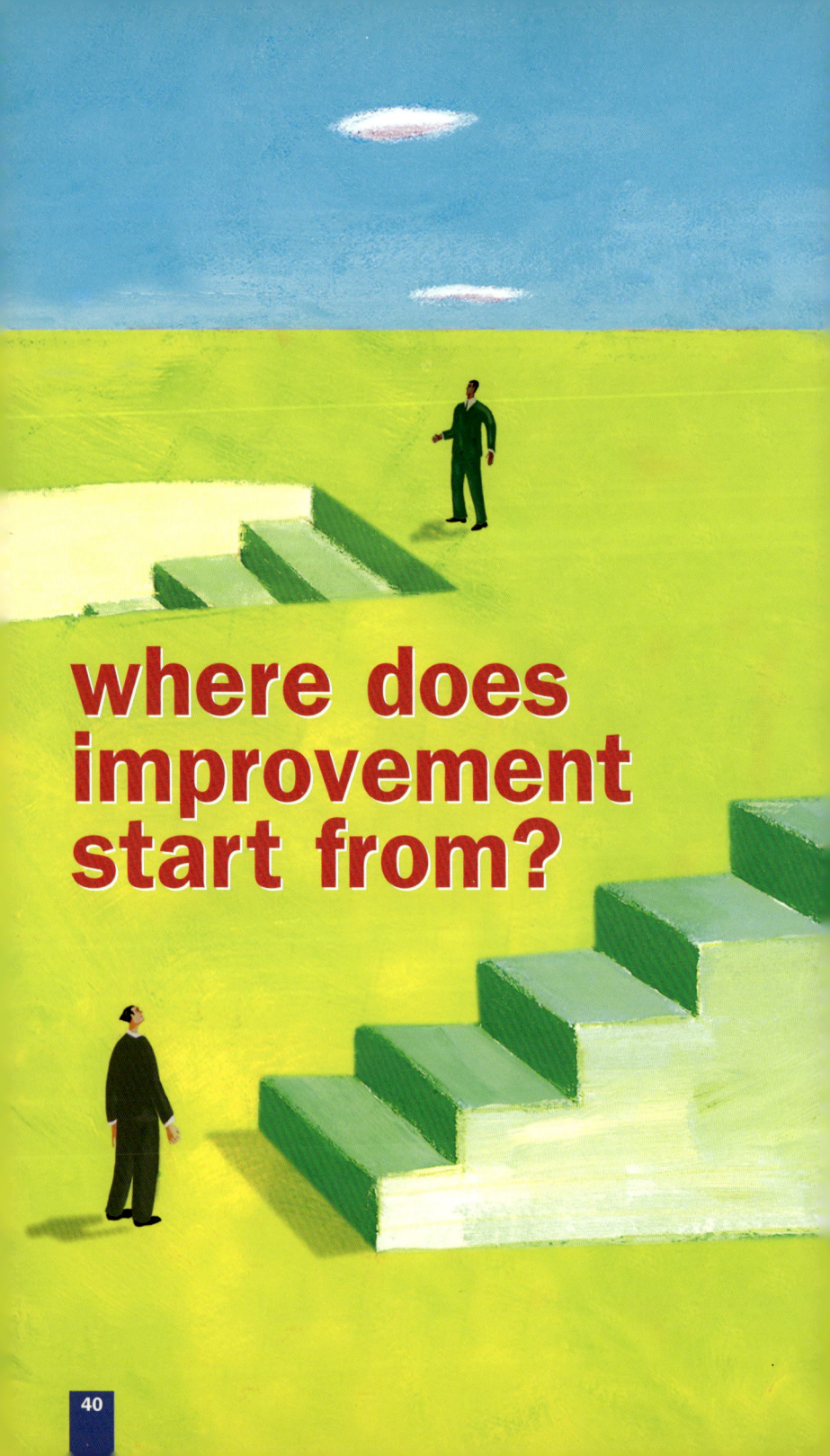

where does improvement start from?

Timed targets may be expressed as a binary (yes/no) condition that has to be fulfilled by a certain date, or there may be more complexity in the sense of increasing levels or steps of performance to be achieved by certain points. This kind of stepped target is particularly useful during far-reaching business change or when aiming for more distant goals.

The baseline

In order to track changes in performance over time, you need a baseline, or starting point from which improvements can be measured. A baseline allows realistic assessment of 'before and after' information; what separates the 'before' and 'after' states can be anything from a radical change to a period of normal business activity during which performance improvement is hoped for. For example, if you had decided to outsource your IT infrastructure provision, you would need to establish just what level of availability and quality is needed in order to assess the third-party provider's service after the change.

Determining the baseline is of great importance to stakeholders who will play a part in achieving improvements or managing change. Their personal performance may depend on the level at which the baseline is set, since it will represent what they have to 'beat' to demonstrate improvement. It may require some discussion to agree exactly what levels of performance it is fair to say are being delivered in the 'before' state.

It is also vital to use measures that have meaning in both 'before' and 'after' states – particularly if they cover a period of far-reaching change. If business processes are radically reengineered, some inputs and outputs may no longer exist in the 'after' state. The baseline, too, may lose its meaning over time, and become perceived as part of the past. Measures that focus on higher levels of the value chain, or on key outputs that are unlikely to change, are those that form the most resilient parts of a good performance framework. These measures will give the truest picture of the benefits of radical change.

Continuous improvement

Often, your aim will not be to reach a specific level of performance, but to achieve continuous improvement.

Targets that demand continuous improvement aim to take into account the benefits that time and experience can bring. The costs of establishing a new business process can be high. As experience increases, lessons are learned and opportunities are perceived, and it should be possible to improve output volumes, quality or efficiency without the need for additional resource or investment. So value for money improves over time.

A continuous improvement target will normally require an increase in savings, reduction in overheads or improvement in quality on a year-on-year or month-on-month basis.

It is easier to quantify continuous improvement at the lower levels of the value chain, but it may also be useful to be able to point to relative or incremental improvements at higher levels. In other words, it may help to generate commitment if you can demonstrate that while the ultimate aim has not been achieved, things are continuously improving and the business is moving in the right direction.

Key questions for setting targets

- Have targets been selected for key activities?

- Are the targets SMART – Specific, Measurable, Achievable, Relevant and Timed?

- Are the targets spread over a range of performance measures, so that you get a balanced picture of what is being achieved?

- Can you be sure that overall performance will not be subverted by the focus on particular targets (perverse incentives)?

- Are the targets challenging? Do they encourage continuous improvement?

- Are requirements for continuous improvement realistic? Do they take account of possible or likely future events?

- Will targets be revised when the performance framework is reviewed?

- Have the consequences of not meeting targets been discussed and considered?

5

gathering and using information

- Regular collection
- Inspections and planned checks
- Principles for collecting information
- Reporting
- Aggregation
- Making comparisons
- Context
- Taking action
- Review

With a balanced, robust and flexible performance framework in place, and performance targets set, performance information can start to be gathered. There are a number of ways to do this, and it is important to define the actual processes that will be used and the responsibilities of those who are involved.

Regular collection

Information can be collected on a regular, routine basis as part of normal working life, or sampled on an ad hoc basis. Some information may be generated automatically by an information system, and other information may need to be logged specially. This information should be made available in a form that is relevant to those who will compare measures to targets and make management decisions.

Inspections and planned checks

Regular inspection keeps business activities under review to ensure that they are working as they should – efficiently and effectively. Processes may also be audited against good practice, or other benchmarks, to ensure that they are complete and operating to a recognised standard.

Planned checks can provide verification that things are working out as planned. They can also highlight where performance measures may not be reflecting the situation 'on the ground' and provide an opportunity for people to raise questions or issues with the performance management system. Planned checks can usefully be linked to reviews of targets, measures, or the entire performance framework.

Customer surveys are another important way to get performance information and feedback on how improvements are seen from outside the business.

Principles for collecting information

- **Keep it focused.** A firm focus will ensure that the right data is collected and irrelevant or repetitious data is avoided, and that the questions posed by the performance measures are answered. Don't collect data because it might be useful at some point in the future.

keep information
focused, flexible,
and meaningful

- **Keep it flexible.** Data should be collected from a variety of sources and through a variety of media, depending on what is best suited to the measure; avoid dependence on one method if you can. Although automation is preferable, manual systems may also be used when they are cost-efficient.

- **Keep it meaningful.** Useful and relevant data can be gathered if the correct measures were set up in the first place. However, data collection should not come to depend on standard checklists as opposed to results-oriented approaches. Data collection must be tailored to the management and reporting needs of the business. To be meaningful, the data collected must contribute, directly or through interpretation, to the business's understanding of itself and its work – organisational learning.

Reporting

Performance information is central to management: decisions should always be based on facts. The main uses for performance information will be to report on performance and to compare performance against targets, but there are others:

- in strategic planning (for example, to identify baselines, gaps, goals and strategic priorities)
- to guide the prioritisation of change initiatives
- in resource allocation decisions
- in day-to-day management of tasks, finances and personnel
- to communicate results to stakeholders
- to examine the business's capabilities against recognised standards.

Performance information must be useful to everyone who needs it. Since there will be a range of uses for the information, there may be a range of users, all with different requirements and priorities. Consulting them in advance will help ensure that what is proposed in terms of reporting will be right for them.

Different stakeholders may also have varying ideas of what constitutes good performance. Stakeholders' definitions of measures and targets must be agreed, otherwise there will be continual debate and counter-productive 'corrective action'.

It may be necessary to tailor the information for different audiences, presenting the most relevant subsets in the most accessible format.

Information directed towards management may have a very different slant to that directed towards customers, since they are interested in different aspects of performance.

Data for external reporting may be required in the form of charts and diagrams, while the same data for day-to-day performance monitoring and management may be required in spreadsheet format to feed into an automatic comparison program. Some results may be suitable for both purposes. For presentation of results, graphical reports will usually make it easier for the recipients to grasp the key messages and draw conclusions.

Internal reports should provide managers with the information they need on key aspects of performance that allow them to assess progress and the achievement of desired business outcomes. The information should aid decisions about future activities and directions. To be useful and appear relevant, reports have to be produced in good time, and reach their audiences quickly.

Exception reporting, where managers receive a brief outline of the instances or periods when performance fell short of targets, is a useful way of drawing attention to measures that warrant special attention.

Aggregation

Aggregation is a way of adding together or combining numerical performance information to produce a single figure that summarises some aspect of performance such as total output or average efficiency.

context will affect performance

Measures in the same units and at the same level can be weighted and added; for example:

- **geographically:** where a single type of measure relating to a single activity at various sites or departments is aggregated across locations to produce regional indicators

- **functionally:** where a single type of measure (like turnaround time) is aggregated across different activities

- **as a composite:** where a number of different types of measure for a single activity are combined into one performance indicator.

Making comparisons

For day-to-day performance management, the information gathered by performance measurement will form the basis of comparison with targets. This will identify whether or not targets are being met.

A minor or short-term deviation from targets should not lead to hasty corrective action. It may be helpful to specify the limits of deviation: what constitutes a serious performance shortfall in terms of nature, magnitude or duration. This will help those carrying out comparisons to determine whether the exception or shortfall is worth reporting or taking action on.

The communication flow between those who measure performance and those who compare measures with targets must be reliable and responsive. Obviously, allocating the two responsibilities to the same team, or the same individual, is ideal – as long as objectivity and impartiality can be maintained.

Performance measurements must be obtained and communicated quickly enough to allow control or remedial action to be undertaken in good time, before the problem worsens. The allowable delay between gathering information and taking action will broadly depend on the level of performance being monitored. For example, correction of day-to-day operational performance will need to be much more responsive than a long-term adjustment of business strategy in response to gradually shifting market conditions.

Context

It is important to remember that the performance framework, balanced and accurate though it may be, is only a representation of a more complex reality. The measurements that fill out the framework are subject to real-world influences, and it is important to take these into account when analysing performance information.

Businesses, departments and contracts are hard to examine in isolation; though nominally discrete, in practice they affect each other in many different ways. The more complex the outputs or outcomes, the more important these interactions become.

Taking the context into account can help to answer questions such as:

- are performance issues the result of factors within the process being examined, or outside it?
- could those responsible for performance reasonably be expected to affect these factors?
- are there any unintended outputs or outcomes – good or bad? Were we responsible for them?
- were we working against existing pressures, or with them?
- were there other factors that prevented the process working well?

Taking action

Performance frameworks should draw attention to success, but they must also highlight areas for improvement. Taking action to improve is a vital part of performance management. Measurement, comparison and analysis are useful tools for learning about a process, but not ends in themselves; they are tools for planning changes and solving problems. It is an important attribute of a good performance framework that it looks at the situation in all its aspects and points the way towards change for the better. Those involved must have the authority to make, or recommend, changes that will affect performance. Without this authority, performance management will lack 'teeth'.

Those who receive performance information must be able (and willing) to use it to make a case for proactive change. As with measuring and comparing, the responsibility for taking action must be clearly allocated, ideally to a single individual. This individual will need the ability and authority to take decisions based on hard facts, coupled with an awareness of the business's culture.

The action taken to improve performance can take different forms and affect different levels of the business. In general, the action to be taken will be of a similar focus to the measure that prompts it.

stay up to speed

For example, a shortfall in output volumes could be remedied by a slight change in inputs, but a failure to achieve key outcomes will require major business change.

Some types of corrective action, with examples, are:

- varying the quantity of the inputs (more investment)
- varying the nature of the inputs (different staff, training for existing staff)
- altering processes (internal reorganisation, changes to infrastructure)
- transforming the process (doing existing tasks differently, outsourcing a service previously provided in-house)
- making changes to related processes and other factors that are clearly affecting performance (changing the context)
- revising unrealistic or unreachable targets
- discarding or replacing inappropriate targets
- creating new incentives, or changing existing ones
- adding new measures and removing those that have not been useful, or that have created perverse incentives.

Small alterations in inputs to a process to remedy output volume problems might happen on a monthly basis and be the responsibility of a single individual – the use of temporary staff to accommodate peaks in workflow, for example.

More significant changes, involving altering outputs or transforming processes in order to affect outcomes, will be undertaken far less frequently (or should be); they will involve more staff and commitment. They will also take effect more slowly – not least because they will almost certainly involve many associated changes to inputs to make them happen.

If major corrective action is to be taken, it could be necessary to revisit performance measures to ensure that they will still be relevant after the changes. Only a continuous picture of performance can tell you whether corrective action has been successful.

Review

It is important to build review into performance management. You also need to consider what contribution performance management is making:

- have you found out what you needed to know?

- should you redefine what constitutes success?

- did you realise the benefits that you wanted? (see chapter 6)

- what can you learn from performance information and its management?

- is performance information being used to enable better decision-making and support the business?

- is the work involved too much trouble for the information gained, or has a modest effort produced interesting and useful results?

- are people happy with the way measures are taken, the people doing the measuring and the targets they have to aim for?

- do people understand why and how performance management benefits the business?

Change is a constant, and the performance framework will need to adapt to new circumstances. This could mean revising targets, choosing new measures or discarding old ones, redefining processes for data collection and analysis. You may even feel that performance information suggests a serious rethink of the direction in which the business is moving.

6

techniques

- Stakeholder analysis
- Benchmarking
- Business Process Reengineering
- Benefits management
- Other techniques

this chapter covers some analytical techniques that can be used in performance management. You need to consider carefully when to use them, as they will not be applicable in every situation, but when appropriate they can be very helpful in quantifying 'soft' factors that are difficult to express numerically. Use techniques to complement your own analysis of the business and the performance framework you create.

Stakeholder analysis

In the context of performance management, a stakeholder is an individual or group of individuals who have an interest in plans and activities because of their direct involvement or because they may be affected by the outcome. Stakeholders can include customers, employees, directors, shareholders, service providers, consultants or other businesses.

Stakeholder analysis means identifying stakeholders and assessing how much of a stake they have, then determining their requirements and expectations. The results inform the choice of measures and targets, and the means by which results are reported.

Identifying stakeholders is as much to do with subjective judgement as analysis. It is often possible to make a case for almost any person or group being a stakeholder, particularly if you expand your focus to those who have influence over less tangible factors such as reputational standing. To keep things focused, identify stakeholders who:

- are personally responsible for achieving outputs or outcomes
- are directly affected by the success or failure of the business process in question
- have a real, direct influence on the business and its operations
- are closely involved in day-to-day business (this could include other businesses)
- control or assign resources
- are widely respected as holding authoritative views and carrying great influence in the business.

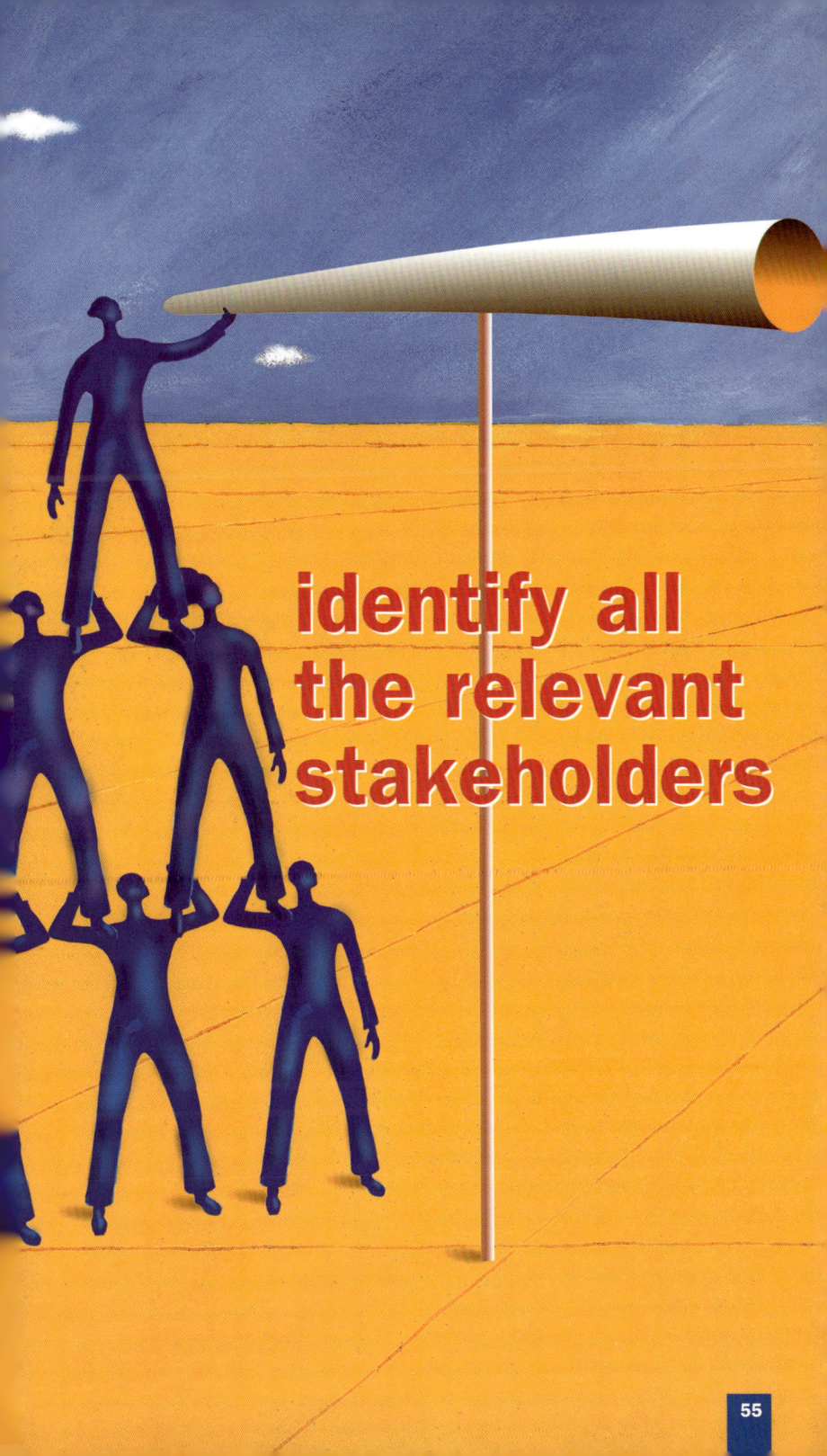

identify all
the relevant
stakeholders

Not all stakeholders are equally important. You will need to consider how much influence they have, how near they are to the business process, and what their 'stake' in it is.

For each important stakeholder, you need to ask 'what are their expectations?' and 'how will they judge performance?' For example, customer expectations for the quality of products and services can be gauged through surveys and questionnaires. It is also important to establish where the expectations of stakeholders are changing – performance requirements in the future may differ from those expressed today.

Benchmarking

Benchmarking is about comparing performance between different businesses, or different departments within a single business. It can be used to:

- bring more objectivity to performance measurement

- highlight areas where improvement is needed

- identify other processes that result in superior performance and could be taken on by the business

- see whether improvements have worked.

Benchmarking can be useful at all levels of the business, from basic processes right up to the performance of the business as a whole. It can focus on costs, standards or results being attained, or processes being used. Benchmarking on costs can be a useful way to determine a fair price for services you buy from other businesses. Process benchmarking is about looking at how others do things – perhaps businesses in a similar area who are not direct competitors.

Whatever the focus, it is vital to compare like with like as far as possible. Cost benchmarking needs to focus on purchases of a similar scale and nature. Process benchmarking needs to focus on processes that are genuinely similar, so that meaningful comparisons can be made and real lessons learned.

In setting up a benchmarking exercise, you need to consider:

- what are your objectives for benchmarking?
- which areas are you going to benchmark?
- what is the baseline against which you will measure improvements?
- how will you get the information that you need?
- how will you analyse and communicate the information?
- how will you use the information to make improvements?

Business Process Reengineering

Business Process Reengineering (BPR) is an approach to bringing about radical change. It is the fundamental rethinking and radical design of business processes to achieve dramatic improvements in measures of performance such as cost, quality, service and speed. It provides a means of delivering major improvements, either identified in business strategies or arising from performance improvement programmes.

BPR principally involves redesigning a business around processes rather than functions. It is a business-led management approach, concentrating on the customer's requirements and the core business processes that deliver against them, rather than on existing hierarchies, management structures or traditions. BPR can be applied in a single department or to the business as a whole.

The benefits of BPR include:

- clearer focus on the customer's needs
- reduced cost of operations
- improved quality of service
- reduced delivery/response times
- improved responsiveness to customer demands.

Whatever the scale, there will be a set of common elements in a BPR exercise. These are summarised below:

- **create customer focus:** activities that support the customer will often cut across business departments or functions, so it is important to stay focused on what will benefit them as well as what suits people within the business
- **rethink functions and processes:** start from what needs to be done to make the business work, rather than what is done at present
- **challenge accepted principles:** assess the reasons for doing things the way you do, and look at the cost and value of activities
- **simplify and discard:** keep only those processes that add value and are absolutely necessary
- **measure performance:** examine the outcome of the BPR exercise through comparisons with a baseline and through benchmarking
- **set audacious objectives:** perhaps some that cannot be achieved by current improvement methods, to encourage adventurous thinking
- **empower people:** provide support for those who will make changes and those who will run the business after the changes.

Benefits management

The outputs and outcomes to be attained through performance management can be specified in terms of the benefits to the business as a whole or stakeholders within it. Analysing performance and improvement in terms of benefits can be a useful way to pinpoint exactly what improvements are needed, and assess whether they have been achieved.

stay up to speed

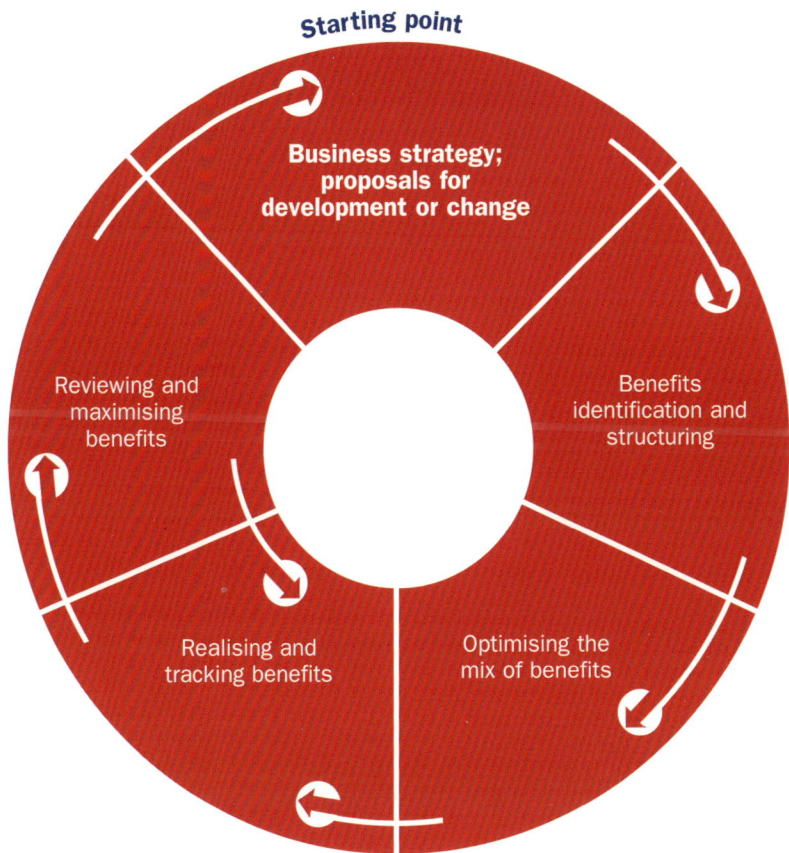

Starting point

Business strategy;
proposals for
development or change

Benefits
identification and
structuring

Reviewing and
maximising
benefits

Optimising the
mix of benefits

Realising and
tracking benefits

The diagram shows the benefits management cycle. The process starts
with the objectives of your business strategy, which may also involve
specific proposals for new developments or changes in the business.
The reasons why these have been identified, and the consequences of
achieving them, will point the way towards the benefits that will result
from them. Benefits fall into three categories:

- those that can be quantified and valued (direct benefits)

- those that can be quantified, but are difficult or impossible to value
  (direct non-financial benefits)

- those that can be identified, but are qualitative and cannot easily
  be quantified (indirect benefits).

If there is a large number of intended benefits, it may be necessary to choose between them or to prioritise them. This is known as 'optimising the benefits mix'. Some trade-off may be necessary, or you may have to delay some planned changes for a while. The options should be considered with as much objectivity as possible – quantifying benefits can help with this.

When you have decided what benefits are expected, their achievement needs to be monitored. This links in with the performance management cycle, since measures and targets should be assigned to individual benefits. When benefits can be quantified, measures can easily be chosen to confirm whether they have been achieved. Non-quantifiable benefits may require subjective evaluation or proxy measures (see chapter 3).

Benefits must be actively managed; they will require close attention to be fully realised. If you decide to use this approach, the responsibility for managing benefits needs to be clearly assigned, and it has to be accepted that this is an ongoing activity, not a one-off exercise.

You also need to be alert to the possibility of benefits that were not expected, or that arise in unexpected ways.

Other techniques

The **Balanced Scorecard** technique, created by Kaplan and Norton, provides a structured approach to setting goals and objectives. It grew from the perception that if performance measurement focused on sales and profits, managers could appear successful in the short term while ignoring the long-term development of the business. The balanced scorecard approach tackles this by looking at ultimate outcomes and long-term concerns, building from the principle that a balanced mix of measures is necessary to represent adequately the full range of business performance. For more details, see *The Balanced Scorecard* by Robert S. Kaplan and David P. Norton (ISBN 0875846513).

The **EFQM Excellence Model** ® defines a framework for business improvement and for measuring that improvement. It is widely used in both the public and private sectors, in the UK and internationally.

The model consists of nine criteria against which the organisation can be assessed, in two categories. Enablers are factors that assess readiness and capability to achieve improvement, while results are comparisons with targets and trends. The model also incorporates innovation and learning, which take the form of feedback from results to enablers.

A major advantage of the model is that it provides a common framework and terminology for people from different backgrounds to compare processes and practices.

The model is © EFQM. The EFQM Excellence Model is a registered trademark. For more information, visit www.efqm.org.

Goal Question Metric was developed by Victor R. Basili and H. Dieter Rombach. It is based on the assumption that for a business to measure performance in a purposeful way it must:

- specify the goals it wishes to achieve
- relate goals to performance data
- create a framework for interpreting the data with respect to the goals.

First, a set of goals is defined. Each goal is then broken down into questions that focus on the achievement of the different aspects of each goal. Finally, metrics (measures) are defined, making a link between the concrete data that will be collected and the questions.

For example, the goal might be to improve the performance of a helpdesk from the perspective of a customer services manager. Questions to ask about this goal, and measures that could be created, might include the following:

- what is the current response time to enquiries?
- average response time
- proportion (percentage) of enquiries answered unacceptably slowly (level to be agreed)
- is the business process of answering enquiries working as well as it could?
- subjective assessment by customer services manager
- perspectives of staff working on the helpdesk
- is the helpdesk improving its performance over time?
- overall improvement in average response time over agreed baseline
- monthly improvements.

Index

stay up to speed